THE RELIGIOUS WRITINGS OF THE FOUNDING FATHERS

Vol. 1, George Washington

Ezra Vaoifi

CONTENTS

INTRODUCTION

Much like Benjamin Franklin, Christopher Columbus, and other greats from the past, the imperfections of George Washington have been highlighted, amplified, and unforgiven by modern historians.

However, Neal A. Maxwell once said that "studying the church through the eyes of its detractors is like interviewing Judas to understand Jesus." The same rings true with the detractors of General George Washington.

If "America's most indispensable man" and "the father of his country" were to return to America today, he would hardly be recognized. He would likely be ridiculed, harassed, and criticized by a band of ungrateful heirs to the country which he

helped establish.

Either way, it is my firm belief that inspired men like George Washington were called of God and prepared by Him to fulfill their important roles. "The American Revolution had its beginning behind the veil," said George A. Smith. "God inspired our fathers to make the Declaration of Independence, and sustained them in their struggles for liberty until they conquered." (Address in the Salt Lake City, 4 July 1854.)

In some cases, the spelling has been slightly modified to fit modern standards. But excluding the chapter titles and bolded headings, the entirety of this text can be ascribed to President George Washington.

To get to know this man, we ought to let him speak for himself...

- E.V.

"THE INVISIBLE HAND"
OUR HEAVENLY FATHER

No people can be bound to acknowledge and adore the invisible hand, which conducts the affairs of men, more than the people of the United States. Every step by which they have advanced to the character of an independent nation seems to have been distinguished by some token of providential agency[1]. (First Inaugural Address, April 30, 1789.)

We may, with a kind of grateful and pious exaltation[2], trace the finger of Providence through those dark and mysterious events, which first induced the States. . . Laying a lasting foundation for tranquility and happiness. . . That the same good Providence may still continue to protect us and prevent us from dashing the cup of national felicity[3] just as it has been lifted to our lips, is the earnest prayer of. . . your faithful friend. (To Jonathan Trumbull Jr., July 20, 1788. *PGW*, Confederation Series, vol. 6, pp. 389-390.)

Supreme and Almighty Being. It is impossible to account for the creation of the Universe without the agency of a Supreme Being. It is impossible to govern the Universe without the aid of a Supreme Being. It is impossible to reason without arriving at a Supreme Being. (Quoted in *Faith and Freedom*, Gingrich, p. 47.)

It would be peculiarly improper to omit, in this first official act, my fervent supplications to that Almighty Being who rules over the universe, who presides in the counsels of nations. (First Inaugural Address, April 30, 1789.)

A superintending Providence is ordering everything for the best, and. . . in due time all will end well. (To Landon Carter, 27 October 1777. *PGW*, Revolutionary War Series, vol. 12, pp. 25–27.)

The Purposes of God.   The determinations of providence are always wise, often inscrutable, and though it's decrees appear to bear hard upon us at times, are nevertheless meant for gracious purposes. (To Bryan Fairfax. March 17, 1778. *PGW*, Revolutionary War Series, vol. 14, pp. 9–11.)

The will of Heaven is not to be controverted or scrutinized by the children of this world. It therefore becomes the creatures of it to submit with patience and resignation to the will of the Creator, whether it be to prolong or to shorten the number of our days, to bless them with health or afflict them with pain. (To George Augustine Washington, 27 January 1793. *PGW*, Presidential Series, vol. 12, pp. 53–54.)

As it has been a kind of destiny that has thrown me upon this service, I shall hope that my undertaking of it is designed to answer some good purpose... I shall rely therefore, confidently, on that Providence which has heretofore preserved and been bountiful to me. (To Martha Washington, 18 June 1775. *PGW*, Revolutionary War Series, vol. 1, pp. 3–6.)

At disappointments and losses which are the effects of Providential acts, I never repine; because I am sure the all-wise Disposer of events knows better than we do, what is best for us, or what we deserve. (To William Pearce, 25 May 1794. *PGW,* Presidential Series, vol. 16, pp. 122–123.)

I thank you for your condolence on the death of my nephew. It is a loss I sincerely regret, but as it is the will of Heaven, whose decrees are always just and wise, I submit to it without a murmur. (To Bryan Fairfax, March 6, 1793. *PGW*, Presidential Series, vol. 12, pp. 271-272.)

God's Hand in Storms. The violent gale[4] which dissipated the two Fleets when on the point of engaging, and the withdrawing. . . to Boston, may appear to us as real misfortunes. But, with you, I consider storms and victory under the direction of a wise Providence who, no doubt, directs them for the best of purposes, and to bring around the greatest degree of happiness to the greatest number of His people. (To Jonathan Trumbull, Sr., 6 September

1778. *PGW,* Revolutionary War Series, vol. 16, pp. 533–534.)

Be Grateful to God.   The hand of Providence has been so conspicuous in all this, that he must be worse than an infidel that lacks faith, and more than wicked, that has not gratitude enough to acknowledge His obligations. (To Brigadier General Thomas Nelson, Jr., 20 August 1778.)

The success which has hitherto attended our united efforts, we owe to the gracious interposition of heaven, and to that interposition let us gratefully ascribe the praise. (Quoted by Ezra T. Benson in "God's Hand in Our Nation's History," 28 March 1977.)

It is the duty of all nations to acknowledge the Providence of Almighty God, to obey His will, to be grateful for His benefits, and humbly to implore His protection and favor. . . that great and glorious Being, who is the beneficent Author of all the good that was, that is, or that will be. That we may then all unite in rendering unto Him our sincere and humble thanks. For His kind care and protection of the people of this country previous to their becoming a nation. For the signal and manifold mercies, and the favorable interpositions of His providence which we experienced in the course and conclusion of the late war. For the great degree of tranquility, union, and plenty, which we have since enjoyed. For the peaceable and rational manner, in which we have been enabled to establish constitutions of government for our safety and happiness, and particularly the national one now lately instituted. For the civil and religious liberty with which we are blessed; and the means we have of acquiring and diffusing useful knowledge; and in general, for all the great and various favors which He hath been pleased to confer upon us. (Thanksgiving Proclamation, October 3, 1789. *PGW*, Presidential Series, vol. 4, pp. 131–132.)

Our Only Dependence. Be assured, gentlemen, that through the many and complicated vicissitudes of an arduous conflict, I have ever turned my eye[5], with a fixed confidence, on that Superintending Providence which governs all events. And the lively gratitude I now feel at the happy termination of our contest is beyond my expression. (To Samuel Phillips, Jr., 10 August 1783. *Founders Online,* National Archives.)

We have. . . abundant reason to thank Providence for its many favorable interpositions in our behalf. It has at times been my only dependence, for all other resources seem to have failed us. (To William Gordon, 9 March 1781.)

I trust in that Providence which has saved us in six troubles, yea in seven, to rescue us again from any imminent, though unseen dangers. Nothing, however, on our part ought to be left undone. (To Benjamin Lincoln, 28 August 1788. *PGW,* Confederation Series, vol. 6, pp.482-482.)

No man has a more perfect reliance on the all wise, and powerful dispensations of the Supreme Being than I have, nor thinks His aid is more necessary. (To William Gordon, May 13, 1776.)

I know the delicate nature of the duties incident to the part which I am called to perform; and I feel my incompetence, without the singular assistance of Providence, to discharge them in a satisfactory manner. . . no fear of encountering difficulties and no dread of losing popularity, shall ever deter me from pursuing what I conceive to be the true interests of my Country. (To the Citizens of Baltimore, 17 April 1789. *PGW*, Presidential Series, vol. 2, pp. 62–65.)

CHRISTIANITY

The Religion of Jesus Christ.   I am a warrior. My words are few and plain, but I will make good what I say. It is my business to destroy all the enemies of these states and to protect their friends. . . You do well to wish to learn our arts and ways of life and above all, the religion of Jesus Christ, which will give you eternal life in the world to come. These will make you a greater and happier people than you are. (To the Chiefs of the Delaware Nation, 12 May 1779; *PGW*, Revolutionary War Series, vol. 20, pp. 447–449.)

"Our Highest Glory"   To the distinguished character of Patriot, it should be our highest glory to add the more distinguished character of *Christian*—The signal Instances of providential goodness which we have experienced and which have now almost crowned our labors with complete Success, demand from us in a peculiar manner the warmest returns of gratitude and piety to the Supreme Author of all Good. (General Orders at Valley Forge, 2 May 1778.)

God Looks Upon The Heart. A true Christian Spirit will lead us to look with compassion upon their errors without insulting them. While we are contending for our own liberty, we should be very cautious of violating the rights of conscience in others. Ever considering that God alone is the judge of the hearts of men and to Him only in this case they are answerable. (To Colonel Benedict Arnold, September 14, 1775. *PGW*, Revolutionary War Series, vol. 1, pp. 455–456.)

HAPPINESS

God Is Invested in Our Happiness. The great Governor of the Universe has led us too long and too far on the road to happiness and glory, to forsake us in the midst of it. (Letter to Benjamin Lincoln, June 29, 1788. *PGW*, vol. 30, p. 11.)

I trust, as you do, that that Providence which has protected all our steps hitherto, will continue to direct them to the consummation[6] of our happiness and prosperity. (To Timothy Pickering, November 3, 1799. *PGW*, Retirement Series, vol. 4, pp. 384–385.)

Happiness Depends Upon Conduct. The pure and benign light of revelation has had a meliorating[7] influence on mankind and increased the blessings of society. At this auspicious period the United States came into existence as a nation. And if their citizens should not be completely free and happy, the fault will be entirely *their own*. . . that it is in their choice and depends upon their *conduct*. Whether they will be respectable and prosperous or contemptible and miserable as a nation. This is the time of their political probation. (To the States, 8 June 1783; Founders Online, National Archives.)

The reflection on the days of difficulty and danger which are past is rendered the more sweet, from a consciousness that they are succeeded by days of uncommon prosperity and security. If we have wisdom to make the best use of the advantages with which we are now favored, we cannot fail (under the just administration of a good Government) to become a great and a happy people. . . May the Father of all mercies scatter light and not darkness in our paths, and make us all in our several vocations useful here, and in His own due time and way, everlastingly happy. (To the Hebrew Congregation in Newport. 18 August 1790. *PGW*, Presidential Series, vol. 6, pp. 284–286.)

Happiness is ours if we have a disposition[8]

to seize the occasion and *make* it our own. (To the States, June 8, 1783; Founders Online, National Archives.)

Virtue and Happiness Inseparably Connected. Can it be that Providence is not connected the permanent felicity of a nation with its virtue? The experiment, at least, is recommended by every sentiment which ennobles human nature. (Farewell Address, September 19, 1796.)

The consideration that human happiness and moral duty are inseparably connected will always continue to prompt me to promote the progress of the former, by inculcating the practice of the latter. (To the Protestant Episcopal Church, 19 August 1789. *PGW*, Presidential Series, vol. 3, pp. 496–499.)

The prospect of national prosperity now before us is truly animating, and ought to excite the exertions of all good men to establish and secure the happiness of their country in the permanent duration of its freedom and independence. America, under the smiles of a Divine Providence, the protection of a good Government, and the cultivation of manners, morals and piety, cannot fail of attaining an uncommon degree of eminence, in literature, commerce, agriculture, improvements at home and respectability abroad. (To Roman Catholics in America, 15 March 1790. *PGW*, Presidential Series, vol. 5, pp. 299–301.)

There is no truth more thoroughly established than that there exists. . . an indissoluble union between virtue and happiness. The propitious smiles of Heaven can never be expected on a nation that disregards the eternal rules of order and right which Heaven itself has ordained. (First Inaugural Address, 1789.)

With a mild constitution and wholesome[9] laws—is it too much to say that our country affords a spectacle of national happiness never surpassed, if ever before equaled, in the annals of human affairs? (Draft of Washington's Seventh Annual Address to Congress, December 1795.)

Happiness is Internal. You ask how I am to be

rewarded for all this? There is one reward that nothing can deprive me of, and that is the consciousness of having done my duty with the strictest rectitude and most scrupulous exactness. (To Lund Washington, *The Writings of George Washington*, ed. Fitzpatrick 18:392.)

Labor to keep alive in your breast that little spark of *celestial fire*, called conscience. (Washington, *Rules of Civility #110*)

Happiness depends more upon the internal frame of a person's own mind, than on the externals in the world. (To Mary Ball Washington, 15 February 1787. *PGW*, Confederation Series, vol. 5, pp. 33–37.)

RELIGION AND MORALITY

Religion and morality are the essential pillars of civil society. I view, with unspeakable pleasure, that harmony and brotherly love [are]. . . the pride of our country and the surest basis of universal harmony. (To William White, 3 March 1797. *Founders Online,* National Archives.)

Right and Wrong Are Eternal.   If the blessings of Heaven showered thick around us should be spilled on the ground or converted to curses, through the fault of those for whom they were intended, it would not be the first instance of folly or perverseness in short-sighted mortals.

The blessed religion revealed in the word of God will remain an eternal and awful monument to prove that the best institutions may be abused by human depravity... in some instances ... to the vilest of purposes...

Let us be honest. Let us be firm. Let us advance directly forward in the path of our duty. Should the path at first prove intricate and thorny, it will grow plain and smooth as we go. In public as in private life, let the eternal line that separates right from wrong, be the fence. (Undelivered First Inaugural Address: Fragments, 30 April 1789. *PGW*, Presidential Series, vol. 2, pp. 158–173.)

May the same wonder-working Deity who, long since delivering the Hebrews from their Egyptian oppressors, planted them in the promised land. . . Whose providential agency has lately been conspicuous in establishing these United States as an independent nation, still continue to water them with the dews of Heaven and to make the inhabitants of every denomination participate in the temporal and spiritual blessings of that people whose God is Jehovah. (To the Savannah Hebrew Congregation, 14 June 1790. *PGW*, Presidential Series, vol. 5, pp. 448–450.)

Be Honest and Just. In politics, as in religion, my tenets are few and simple. The leading one of which (and indeed that which embraces most others) is to be honest and just ourselves . . . when there is disorder within, it will appear without. And sooner or later will shew itself in acts. (To James Anderson, December 24, 1795. *PGW*, Presidential Series, vol. 19, pp. 290–294.)

Faith Without Works is Dead.   [It is] much to be lamented that our endeavors do not at all times accord with our wishes. Each State is anxious to see the end of our Warfare accomplished, but shrinks when it is called upon for the means! And either withholds them altogether or grants them in such a way as to defeat the end. . . if the States can not or will not rouse to more vigorous exertions, they must submit to the consequences.

Providence has done much for us in this contest, but we must do something for *ourselves*, if we expect to go triumphantly through with it. (To James McHenry, 12 March / 18 July 1782. *Founders Online,* National Archives.)

America Offers an Advantage to the Virtuous. The spirit of the Religions and the genius of the political Institutions of this Country must be an inducement. Under a good government (which I have no doubt we shall establish) this Country certainly promises greater advantages, than almost any other, to persons. . . who are *determined to be sober, industrious and virtuous members* of Society. (To Francis Adrian Van der Kemp, 28 May 1788. *PGW,* vol.6, pp. 300-301.)

Important Learned *and* Virtuous. Pursue your studies closely. . . conduct yourselves, on all occasions, with decency and propriety. . . every hour misspent is lost forever—and that future years cannot compensate for lost days at this period of your life. This reflection must shew the necessity of an unremitting application to your studies.. . . a good moral character is the first essential in a man, and that the habits contracted[17] at your age are generally indelible[18], and your conduct here may stamp your character through life. It is therefore highly important that you should endeavor not only to be learned but *virtuous*. (To George Steptoe Washington, December 5,1790. *PGW*, Presidential Series, vol. 7, pp. 31–34.)

True Patriots Don't Overthrow Religion. Of all the dispositions and habits which lead to political prosperity, religion and morality are indispensable supports. In *vain* would that man claim the tribute of patriotism, who should labor to *subvert* these great pillars of human happiness. . . The mere politician, equally with the pious man, ought to respect and to cherish them. A volume could not trace all their connections with private and public felicity. (Washington's Farewell Address, 1796.)

Morality Cannot Survive Without Religion. Let us with caution indulge the supposition that morality can be maintained without religion. Whatever may be conceded to the influence of refined education on minds of peculiar structure, reason and experience both forbid us to expect that national morality can prevail in *exclusion* of religious principle. . . 'Tis substantially true, that virtue or morality is a necessary spring of popular government. (Washington's Farewell Address, 1796.)

"Love Thy Neighbor As Thyself " The interests of a nation, when well understood, will be found to coincide with their moral duties. Among these, it is important to cultivate peace and friendship with our neighbors. (Draft of Fourth Annual Address to Congress, 1792; *PAH*, vol. 12, pp. 558–566.)

Let the wise and the virtuous unite their efforts to reclaim the misguided and to detect and defeat the arts of the factious.[19] The union of good men is a basis on which the security of our internal peace and the stability of our Government may safely rest. It will always prove an adequate rampart against the vicious and disorderly. (To the citizens of Carlisle, PA. October 6, 1794. *PGW*, Presidential Series, vol. 17, pp. 14–18.)

Let your heart feel for the affliction and distresses of everyone; and let your hand give in proportion to your purse, remembering always the estimation of the widow's mite. (To Bushrod Washington, January 15, 1783. *Founders Online*, National Archives)

Never let an indigent[20] person ask, without receiving something, if you have the means; always recollecting in what light the widow's mite was viewed. (To George Washington Parke Custis, 15 November 1796. *Founders Online*, National Archives.)

Choose Your Friends Wisely. Associate yourself with men of good quality if you esteem your own reputation. For it is better to be *alone* than in bad company. (Washington, *Rules of Civility*, #56)

Prudence, wisdom, and patriotism were never more essentially necessary than at the present moment. Though I prize, as I ought, the good opinion of my fellow citizens. . . I would not seek or retain popularity at the expense of one social duty or moral virtue.

While doing what my conscience informed me was right as it respected my God, my country, and myself, I could despise all the party clamor and unjust censure, which must be expected from some, whose personal enmity might be occasioned by their hostility to the government. (To Henry Lee, Jr., 22 September 1788. *PGW*, Confederation Series, vol. 6, pp. 528–531.)

A slender acquaintance with the world must convince every man that *actions*, not words, are the true criterion of the attachment of his friends, and that the most liberal professions of goodwill are very far from being the surest marks of it. (To Major General John Sullivan. *PGW*, Revolutionary War Series, vol. 23, pp. 625–626.)

Truth Will Prevail. In the progress of morality and science, to which our government will give every furtherance[21], we may confidently expect the advancement of true religion, and the completion of our happiness. (To the Presbyterian Ministers of Massachusetts, November 2, 1789. *PGW*, Presidential Series, vol. 4, pp. 274–277.)

Truth will ultimately prevail, where there are

pains taken to bring it to light. (To Charles M. Thruston, August 10, 1794.)

Stand Up for Truth.   General Lee's publication. . . puts me in a disagreeable Situation. . . he has most barefacedly misrepresented facts in some places, and thrown out insinuations in others that have not the smallest foundation in truth. Not to attempt a refutation is [an] acknowledgement of the justice of his assertions. For though there are thousands who know how unsupported his piece is, there are yet tens of thousands that know nothing of the matter and will be led naturally to conclude that bold and confident assertions, uncontradicted, must be founded in truth. (To Joseph Reed, December 12, 1778. *PGW*, Revolutionary War Series, vol. 18, pp. 396–398.)

Religion is as necessary to reason as reason is to religion. The one cannot exist without the other. (Mead, *12,000 Inspirational Quotes*, p.374)

Elect Leaders Out of Principal, Not Party.   It is. . . most devoutly to be wished that faction[22] were at an end, and that those to whom everything dear and valuable is entrusted would lay aside party views and return to first principles. Happy, happy, thrice happy [would be] our country if such were the government. . . We are not to expect that the path is to be strewed with flowers. That great and good Being who rules the universe has disposed matters otherwise, and for wise purposes, I am persuaded. (To Joseph Reed, November 27, 1778. *PGW*, Revolutionary War Series, vol. 18, pp. 316–317.)

AMERICA – A CHOICE LAND

God Will Preserve This Land. If we had a secret resource of a nature unknown to our enemy, it was in the unconquerable resolution of our citizens, the conscious rectitude of our cause, and a confident trust that *we should not be forsaken* by Heaven. . . (Undelivered First Inaugural Address: Fragments, 30 April 1789. *PGW*, Presidential Series, vol. 2, pp. 158–173.)

It is indeed a pleasure. . . to view in retrospect all the meanderings[10] of our past labors; the difficulties through which we have waded, and the fortunate haven to which the ship has been brought! Is it possible after this that it should founder? Will not the all-wise and all-powerful Director of human events preserve it? I think He will. (To Jonathan Trumbull, Sr., 15 May 1784. *PGW*, Confederation Series, vol. 1, p. 385.)

America To Be Beautified. I feel the consolatory joys of futurity in contemplating the immense deserts, yet untrodden by the foot of man, soon to become fair as the garden of God, soon to be animated by the activity of multitudes and soon to be made vocal with the praises of the Most High. (Undelivered First Inaugural Address: Fragments, 30 April 1789. *PGW*, Presidential Series, vol. 2, pp. 158–173.)

The Discovery of America Was Divinely Directed. Can it be imagined that so many peculiar advantages of soil and of climate for agriculture and for navigation were lavished in vain? Or that this continent was not *created and reserved*, so long *undiscovered*, as a theatre for those glorious displays of Divine Munificence?

The salutary[11] consequences of which shall flow to another hemisphere and extend through the interminable series of ages! Should not our souls exult[12] in the prospect? Though I shall not survive to perceive with these bodily senses, but a small portion of the blessed effects which our revolution will occasion in the rest of the world; yet I enjoy the progress of human society and human happiness in anticipation. I rejoice in a belief that intellectual light will spring up in the dark corners of the earth. (Undelivered First Inaugural Address: Fragments, 30 April 1789. *PGW*, Presidential Series, vol. 2, pp. 158–173.)

Designated for Greatness. The Citizens of America, placed in the most enviable condition... They are from this period to be considered as the Actors, on a most conspicuous theatre, which seems to be peculiarly designated by Providence for the display of human greatness and felicity. Here they are not only surrounded with everything which can contribute to the completion of private and domestic enjoyment, but Heaven has crowned all its other blessings by giving a fairer opportunity for political happiness than any other nation has ever been favored with. (To the States, 8 June 1783; Founders Online, National Archives.)

Our Location Helps Us Avoid War. As for us, we are plodding on in the dull road of peace and politics. We, who live in these ends of the earth, only hear of the rumors of war, like the roar of distant thunder. It is to be hoped, our remote local situation will prevent us from being swept into its vortex. (To Chastellux, 25 April, 1788. *PGW*, vol. 6, pp. 227-230.)

America Will Never Yield To Anarchy. The most gracious Being, who hath hitherto watched over the interests and averted the perils of the United States, will never suffer so fair an inheritance to become a prey to anarchy, despotism, or any other species of oppression. (To the Mayor, Recorder, Aldermen, and Common Council of Philadelphia, 20 April 1789. *PGW*, Presidential Series, vol. 2, pp. 83–84.)

I earnestly pray that the Omnipotent Being, who hath not deserted the cause of America in the hour of its most extreme hazard, will never yield so fair a heritage of freedom a prey to anarchy or despotism. (To James McHenry, 31 July 1788. *PGW*, Confederation Series, vol. 6, pp. 409–410.)

OUR DUTY AS CITIZENS

Emulating the Savior Makes Better Citizens.
I now make it my earnest prayer, that God would
have you, and the state over which you preside, in
His holy protection, that he would incline hearts
of the citizens to cultivate a spirit of subordination and obedience to government, to entertain
a brotherly affection and love for one another, for
their fellow citizens of the United States at large,
and particularly for their brethren who have served
in the field, and finally, that He would most graciously be pleased to dispose us to all, to do justice,
to love mercy, and to demean ourselves with that
charity, humility and pacific temper of mind, which
were the characteristics of the divine Author of our
blessed religion, and without an humble imitation
of whose example in these things, we can never

hope to be a happy nation. (To the States, June 14, 1783.)

While we are zealously performing the duties of good citizens and soldiers we certainly ought not to be inattentive to the higher duties of religion—To the distinguished character of Patriot, it should be our highest glory to add the more distinguished character of Christian—The signal Instances of providential goodness which we have experienced and which have now almost crowned our labors with complete success, demand from us in a peculiar manner the warmest returns of gratitude and piety to the Supreme Author of all Good. (General Orders at Valley Forge, 2 May 1778.)

Go to Church.   You ought to have been at church, praying as becomes every good Christian man who has as much to answer for as you have. Strange it is that you will be so blind to truth that the enlightening sounds of the Gospel cannot reach your ear, nor no examples awaken you to a sense of goodness.

Could you but behold with what religious zeal I [hasten] to church on every Lord's Day, it would do your heart good, and fill it, I hope, with equal fervency. (To Burwell Bassett, 28 August 1762. *PGW*, Colonial Series, 7:147–148.)

True Religion. While justice protects all in their religious rights, true religion affords government its surest support. (Letter to the Reformed Dutch Church, October 9, 1789)

While all men within our territories are protected in worshipping the Deity according to the dictates of their consciences; it is rationally to be expected from them in return, that they will be emulous of evincing the sincerity of their profession by the innocence of their lives, and the beneficence of their actions: For no man, who is profligate[13] in his morals, or a bad member of the civil community, can possibly be a true Christian, or a credit to his own religious society. (To the General Assembly of the Presbyterian Church. *PGW,* vol.2, pp.420-422.)

Be Grateful to God. When we review the calamities which afflict so many other nations, the present condition of the United States affords. . . unexampled prosperity of all classes of our Citizens. . . Circumstances which peculiarly mark our situation with indications of the Divine Beneficence towards us.

In such a state of things it is. . . our duty as a people, with devout reverence and affectionate gratitude, to acknowledge our many and great obligations to Almighty God and to implore Him to continue and confirm the blessings we experience.

Deeply penetrated with this sentiment, I, George Washington, President of the United States, do recommend to all Religious Societies and Denominations and to all persons whomsoever within the United States to set apart and observe Thursday the nineteenth day of February next as a day of public thanksgiving and prayer. And on that day, to meet together and render their sincere and hearty thanks to the Great Ruler of nations for the manifold and signal mercies which distinguish our lot as a nation. Particularly for the possession of constitutions of government which unite and, by their union, establish liberty with order. For the preservation of our peace, foreign and domestic. . . and generally for the prosperous course of our affairs public and private.

And at the same time humbly and fervently to beseech the kind Author of these blessings graciously to prolong them to us. To imprint on our hearts a deep and solemn sense of our obligations to Him for them. To teach us rightly to estimate their immense value. To preserve us from the arrogance of prosperity, and from hazarding the advantages we enjoy by delusive pursuits. To dispose us to merit the continuance of His favors by not abusing them. By our gratitude for them and by a correspondent conduct as citizens (and as men) to render this country more and more a safe and propitious asylum for the unfortunate of other countries.

To extend among us true and useful knowledge. To diffuse and establish habits of sobriety, order, morality, and piety. And finally, to impart all the blessings we possess, or ask for ourselves, to the whole family of mankind. (Proclamation, 1 January 1795. *PGW*, Presidential Series, vol. 17, pp. 354–358.)

It having pleased of the Almighty Ruler of the universe propitiously to defend the cause of the united American states... It becomes us to set apart day for gratefully acknowledging the divine goodness and celebrating the important events which we owe to His benign intervention. (General Orders, 5 May 1778. *PGW*, Revolutionary War Series, vol. 15, pp. 38–41.)

I must be permitted to consider the wisdom and unanimity of our national councils, the firmness of our citizens, and the patience and bravery of our Troops, which have produced so happy a termination of the War, as the most conspicuous effect of the Divine interposition... No occasion may offer more suitable than the present to express my humble thanks to God. (To Elias Boudinot, 26 August 1783. *Founders Online,* National Archives.)

This singular favor[14] of Providence is to be received with thankfulness, and the happy moment which Heaven has pointed out for the firm establishment of American Liberty ought to be embraced with becoming spirit. (To General James Potter, 18 October 1777. *PGW*, Revolutionary War Series, 11:547.)

Defend Liberty. My highest ambition is to be the happy instrument of vindicating[15] those rights, and to see this devoted province[16] again restored to peace, liberty and safety... I earnestly implore that Divine Being in whose hands are all human events, to make you... distinguished in private and public happiness. (To the Massachusetts Provincial Congress, July 4, 1775. *PGW,* Revolutionary War Series, vol. 1, pp. 59–60.)

Multiply and Replenish the Earth. I wish to see the sons and daughters of the world in peace and busily employed in the more agreeable amusement of fulfilling the first and great commandment—*Increase and Multiply.*

As an encouragement to which we have opened the fertile plains of the Ohio to the poor, the needy and the oppressed of the Earth. Anyone, therefore, who is heavy laden or who wants land to cultivate may repair thither and abound, as in the land of promise with milk and honey. (To Lafayette, 25 July 1785. *PGW*, Confederation Series, 3:151–155.)

WICKEDNESS

Lack of Virtue in the States.   I think often of our situation, and view it with concern. From the high ground on which we stood, from the plain path which invited our footsteps, to be so fallen! So lost! It is really mortifying. But virtue, I fear, has, in a great degree taken its departure from our land. And the want[23] of disposition to do justice is the source of the national embarrassments. (To John Jay, 18 May 1786. *PGW*, Confederation Series, vol. 4, pp. 55–56.)

Pride.   How pitiful, in the eye of reason and religion, is that false ambition which desolates the world with fire and sword for the purposes of conquest and fame; when compared to the milder virtues of making our neighbors and our fellow men as happy as their. . . natures will permit them to be! (To John Lathrop, 22 June 1788. *PGW*, vol. 6, pp.

338-339.)

Gambling. Avoid gaming.[24] This is a vice which is productive of every possible evil, equally injurious to the morals and health of its votaries. It is the child of avarice, the brother of iniquity, and the father of mischief. It has been the ruin of many worthy families, the loss of many a man's honor, and the cause of suicide.

To all those who enter the list, it is equally fascinating; the successful gamester pushed his good fortune till it is overtaken by a reverse; the losing gamester, in hopes of retrieving past misfortunes, goes on from bad to worse, till, grown desperate, he pushes at everything and loses his all. . . Few gain by this abominable practice, while thousands are injured. (To Bushrod Washington, January 15, 1783. *Founders Online*, National Archives.)

I have, both by threats and persuasive means, endeavored to discountenance gaming, drinking, swearing, and irregularities of every other kind. While I have, on the other hand, practiced every artifice to inspire a laudable emulation in the Officers for the service of their country; and to encourage the Soldiers in the unerring exercise of their duty. (To Robert Dinwiddie, 18 April 1756. *PGW*, Colonial Series, vol. 3, pp. 13–15.)

A Drunkard No Different Than Wild Beast. I [exhort] you to refrain from spirituous liquors. They will prove your ruin if you do not. Consider how little a drunken Man differs from a beast. The latter is not endowed with reason, the former *deprives* himself of it. And when that is the case, acts like a brute, annoying and disturbing everyone around him.

But this is not all, nor. . . the worst of it. By degrees it renders a person feeble and not only unable to serve others, but to help himself. And being an act of his own, he falls from a state of usefulness into contempt and at length suffers, if not perishes in penury and want.

Don't let this be your case.

Shew yourself more of a man and a Christian

than to yield to so intolerable a vice. Which cannot, to the greatest lover of liquor, give more pleasure to sip in the poison, for it is no better. (To John Christian Ehlers, 23 December 1793. *PGW*, Presidential Series, vol. 14, pp. 596–598.)

Good Friends Help You Avoid Sin.   When you have leisure to go into company it should always be of the best kind that the place you are in will afford; by this means you will be constantly improving your manners and cultivating your mind ...

If you comply with the advice herein given ... and employ your time of relaxation in proper company, you will find but few opportunities and little inclination... to enter into those scenes of vice and dissipation[25] which too often present themselves to youth in every place...

[F]or you must be employed, and if it is not in pursuit of those things which are *profitable* it must be in pursuit of those which are *destructive.* (To George Steptoe Washington, 23 March 1789. *PGW*, Presidential Series, vol. 1, pp. 438–441.)

Few men have virtue to withstand the highest bidder. (*PGW*, vol.22, pp. 160-161.)

Swearing Condemned.   The General is sorry to be informed that the foolish and wicked practice of profane cursing and swearing (a vice heretofore little known in an American army) is growing into fashion.

[H]e hopes the officers will, by example as well as influence, endeavor to check it. . . we can have little hopes of the blessing of Heaven on our arms, if we insult it by our impiety[26] and folly . . . it is a vice so mean and low. . . that every man of sense and character detests and despises it. (General Orders, 3 August 1776. *PGW*, Revolutionary War Series, vol. 5, pp. 551–552.)

Ingratitude.   Nothing is a greater stranger to my breast, or a sin that my soul more abhors, than that black and detestable one, *ingratitude*. (To Robert Dinwiddie, 29 May 1754. *PGW*, Colonial Series, vol. 1, pp. 107–115.)

Slavery.   There is not a man living who wished

more sincerely than I do to see a plan adopted for the abolition of [slavery]; But there is only one proper and effectual mode by which it can be accomplished, and that is by legislative authority. (To Robert Morris, 1786.)

Your... view of emancipating the slaves... is a generous and noble proof of your humanity. Would to God a like spirit would diffuse itself generally into the minds of the people of this country, but I despair of seeing it. Some petitions were presented to the [Virginia] Assembly at it's last session, but they could scarcely obtain a reading. To set [the slaves] afloat at once would, I really believe, be productive of much inconvenience and mischief. But by degrees it certainly might, and assuredly ought to be effected. (To Marquis de Lafayette, 1786.)

I never mean... to possess another slave by purchase, it being among my first wishes to see some plan adopted by which slavery in this country may be abolished. (To John Francis Mercer, 1786.)

I wish from my soul that the legislature of this

state [Virginia] could see the policy of a gradual abolition of slavery. It would prevent much future mischief. (To Lawrence Lewis, 1797.)

I can clearly foresee that nothing but the rooting out of slavery can perpetuate the existence of our Union, by consolidating it in a sold bond of principal. (To John Bernard, 1798.)

Benedict Arnolds Treason. Treason of the blackest dye was yesterday discovered! General Arnold who commanded at Westpoint... was about to deliver up that important post into the hands of the enemy. Such an event must have given the American cause a deadly wound, if not a fatal stab. Happily the treason has been timely discovered to prevent the fatal misfortune.

The Providential train of circumstances which led to it affords the most convincing proof that the liberties of America are the object of divine protection...

Our enemies (despairing[27] of carrying their point by force) are practicing every base art[28] to effect by bribery and corruption what they cannot accomplish in a manly way. (General Orders, 26 September 1780.)

In no instance since the commencement of the War has the interposition of Providence appeared more conspicuous than in the rescue of the post and garrison[29] of West point from Arnolds villainous perfidy.[30]

A combination of extraordinary circumstances: An unaccountable deprivation of presence of mind in a man of the first abilities, and the virtuous conduct of three Militia Men. [These acts] threw the adjutant General of the British forces in America, with full proofs of Arnold's treachery, into our hands. . . At this time, Arnold is undergoing the torments of a mental Hell. (To John Laurens, 13 October 1780. *Founders Online,* National Archives.)

GENERAL ORDERS

(TO THE TROOPS, 1775 – 1783)

Importance of Moral Character. Purity of morals [is] the only sure foundation of public happiness in any country and highly conducive to order, subordination and success in an army. (General Orders, 21 October 1778. *PGW*, Revolutionary War Series, vol. 17, pp. 493–494.)

All officers, non-commissioned officers and soldiers are positively forbid from playing at cards, and other games of chance; At this time of public distress, men may find enough to do *in the service of their God*, and their country, without abandoning themselves to vice and immorality. (General Orders, 26 February 1776. *PGW*, Revolutionary War Series, vol. 3, p. 362.)

The blessing and protection of Heaven are at

all times necessary, but especially so in times of public distress and danger. The General hopes and trusts that every officer, and man, will endeavor so to live, and act, as becomes a Christian Soldier defending the dearest rights and liberties of his country. . . (General Orders, 9 July 1776. *PGW*, Revolutionary War Series, vol. 5, pp. 245–247.)

Victory is in God's Hands. The time is now near at hand which must probably determine, whether Americans are to be Freemen or Slaves. Whether they are to have any property they can call their own, whether their Houses, and Farms, are to be pillaged and destroyed, and they consigned to a State of Wretchedness from which no *human* efforts will probably deliver them.

The fate of unborn millions will now depend, under God, on the courage and conduct of this army. Our cruel and unrelenting enemy leaves us no choice but a brave resistance, or the most abject submission. This is all we can expect.

We have, therefore, to resolve to *conquer or*

die... Let us therefore rely upon the goodness of the cause, and the aid of the Supreme Being, in whose hands victory is, to animate and encourage us to great and noble Actions... a freeman contending for liberty on his own ground is superior to any slavish mercenary on earth. (General Orders, 2 July 1776. *PGW*, Revolutionary War Series, vol. 5, pp. 179–182.)

Prepare the Mind.   The season is now fast approaching, when every man must expect to be drawn into the field of action, it is highly necessary that he should prepare his mind, as well as everything necessary for it. It is a noble cause we are engaged in. It is the cause of virtue and mankind. Every temporal advantage and comfort to us, and our posterity, depends upon the vigor of our exertions.

In short, freedom or slavery must be the result of our conduct...

Next to the favor of Divine Providence, nothing is more essentially necessary to give this Army the victory of all it's enemies, than exactness of discipline... (General Orders, 27 February 1776. *PGW*, Revolutionary War Series, vol. 3, pp. 379–381.)

The General flatters himself, that every man's *mind* and arms are now prepared for the glorious contest, upon which so much depends...

We must resolve to conquer, or die. With this resolution and the blessing of Heaven, victory and success certainly will attend us. (General Orders, 14 August 1776. *PGW*, Revolutionary War Series, vol. 6, pp. 17–18.)

To be *well prepared* for an engagement is, under God – whose divine aid it behooves us to supplicate[31] – more than one half the battle. (General Orders, 30 June 1776. *PGW*, Revolutionary War Series, vol. 5, pp. 154–157.)

Appreciation to God Expected of Soldiers. The Commander in Chief is confident [that] the Army under his immediate direction will shew their gratitude to Providence, for thus favoring the cause of freedom and America; and by their thankfulness to God, their zeal and perseverance in this righteous cause, continue to deserve His future blessings. (General Orders, 14 November 1775. *PGW*, Revolutionary War Series, vol. 2, pp. 369–370.)

The signal Instances of providential goodness which we have experienced and which have now almost crowned our labors with complete Success, demand from us in a peculiar manner the warmest returns of gratitude and piety to the Supreme Author of all Good. (General Orders at Valley Forge, 2 May 1778)

The General hopes such frequent favors from divine providence will animate every American to continue to exert his utmost in the defense of the liberties of his country, as it would now be basest ingratitude to the Almighty and to their country, to show... the least backwardness in the public cause. (General Orders, 28 November 1775. *PGW*, Revolutionary War Series, vol. 2, pp. 443–444.)

Pray for Victory in War. Whereas it becomes

us humbly to approach Almighty God with gratitude and praise for the wonders which His goodness
has wrought in conducting our forefathers to this
western world, protecting them and their posterity
and raising us, their children, from deep distress to
be numbered among the nations of the Earth.

[He] hath prospered our arms and those of our
ally, shielded our troops in the hour of danger and
led them to victory. . . He went forth with them
against the savage tribes...

He hath prospered our commerce, given success to those who have fought the enemy on the face
of the deep, and above all that He hath diffused the
glorious light of the Gospel.

Therefore, [it is] recommended to the several
States to appoint Thursday the ninth of December
next to be a day of public and solemn Thanksgiving to Almighty God for His mercies. And of prayer
for the continuance of His favor and protection to
these United States.

To beseech His gracious influence on our public councils, that He would go forth with our hosts and crown our arms with victory, grant the plentiful effusions of divine grace to His church, bless and prosper the means of education, and spread the light of Christianity through the Earth...

That He would be graciously pleased to turn the hearts of our enemies and dispense the blessings of peace to contending nations.

That He would in mercy pardon our sins and receive us into His favor, and finally that He would *establish the Independence of these United-States upon the basis of religion and virtue*, and support and protect them in the enjoyment of peace, liberty and safety.

A strict observance to be paid by the Army to this proclamation and the Chaplains are to prepare and deliver discourses suitable to it. (General Orders, 27 November 1779. *PGW*, Revolutionary War Series, vol. 23, pp. 442–444.)

The General commands all officers, and soldiers, to pay strict obedience to the Orders of the

Continental Congress, and by their unfeigned, and pious observance of their religious duties, incline the Lord, and Giver of Victory, to prosper our arms. (General Orders, 15 May 1776. *PGW*, Revolutionary War Series, vol. 4, pp. 305–306.)

LETTERS DURING THE WAR

Washington's Title of Liberty. The Colonies, confiding in the justice of their cause and the purity of their intentions, have reluctantly appealed to that Being in whose Hands are all human Events. He has hitherto smiled upon their virtuous Efforts. . . Come then, my Brethren, unite with us in an indissoluble Union, let us run together to the same goal.

We have taken up Arms in Defense of our Liberty, our Property, our Wives, and our Children. We are determined to preserve them, or die.

We look forward with Pleasure to that Day not far remote (we hope) when the Inhabitants of America shall have one Sentiment, and the full Enjoyment of the Blessings of a free Government. . . the Grand American Congress have sent an Army into your Province. . . not to plunder, but to protect you; To animate and bring forth into action those sentiments of Freedom you have disclosed. . .

Let no Man desert his Habitation—Let no one flee as before an Enemy. The Cause of America, and of Liberty, is the Cause of every virtuous American Citizen; Whatever may be his Religion or his Descent, the United Colonies know no Distinction but such as Slavery, Corruption and arbitrary Domination may create.

Come then, ye generous Citizens, range yourselves under the *Standard of general Liberty*—against which all the force and artifice of tyranny will never be able to prevail. (To the Inhabitants of Canada. September 14, 1775. *PGW*, Revolutionary War Series, vol. 1, pp. 461–463.)

I remonstrated with you, on the unworthy treatment shewn to the . . . citizens of America. . . our virtuous Citizens, whom the hand of tyranny has forced into arms, to defend their wives, their children, and their property . . . I now avail myself of those advantages which the sacred cause of my country, of liberty, and human nature give me over you. (To General Thomas Gage of the British Army. August 19, 1775. *PGW*, Revolutionary War Series, vol. 1, pp. 326–328.)

Never Been a Greater Cause. It is easier to conceive than to describe the situation of my mind for some time past, and my feelings under our present circumstances. Search the vast volumes of history through, and I much question whether a case similar to ours is to be found...

How it will end, God in His great goodness will direct. I am thankful for His protection to this time. (To Joseph Reed. 4 January 1776. *PGW*, Revolutionary War Series, vol. 3, pp. 23–27.)

We must now determine to be enslaved or free. If we make freedom our choice, we must obtain it by the blessing of Heaven on our united and vigorous efforts... and I trust Providence will smile on our efforts, and establish us once more the inhabitants of a free and happy country. (To the Pennsylvania Associators, 8 August 1776. *PGW*, Revolutionary War Series, vol. 5, pp. 637–638.)

This singular favor of Providence is to be received with thankfulness, and the happy moment which Heaven has pointed out for the firm establishment of American Liberty ought to be embraced with becoming spirit. (To Brigadier General James Potter, 18 October 1777. *PGW*, Revolutionary War Series, 11:547.)

The God of Armies. The designs of the enemy are not, as yet, clearly unfolded. But I believe that Philadelphia is the object in view. This, however, may or may not be the case...

That the God of Armies may enable me to bring the present contest to a speedy and happy conclusion, thereby gratifying me in a retirement to the calm and sweet enjoyment of domestic happiness, is the fervent prayer, and most ardent wish of my soul. (To Edmund Pendleton, April 12, 1777. *PGW*, Revolutionary War Series, 9:140–141.)

Gratitude to God. You speak the language of my heart, in acknowledging the magnitude of our obligations to the Supreme Director of all human events...

For my own part, gentlemen, in whatever situation I shall be hereafter, my supplications will ever ascend to Heaven, for the prosperity of my Country in general, and for the individual happiness of those who are attached to the Freedom, and Independence of America. (To Philip Nagel, 1 December 1783. *Founders Online,* National Archives.)

Providence has a just claim to my humble, and grateful thanks for its protection and direction of me, through the many difficult and intricate scenes which this contest hath produced; and for it's constant interposition in our behalf when the clouds were heaviest, and seemed ready to burst upon us.

To paint the distresses and perilous situation of this army in the course of last winter for want of clothes, provisions, and almost every other necessary essential to the well-being (I may say existence) of an Army, would require more time, and an abler pen than mine. Nor (since our prospects have so miraculously brightened) shall I attempt it, or even bear it in remembrance, further than as a memento of what is due to the Great Author of all the care and good that has been extended in relieving us in difficulties and distress. (To Landon Carter, 30 May 1778. *PGW*, Revolutionary War Series, 15:267–270.)

I have often thought how much happier I should have been, if, instead of accepting command under such circumstances I had taken my musket upon my shoulder and entered the ranks. Or (if I could have justified the measure to posterity and my own conscience) had retired to the back country...

If I shall be able to rise superior to[32] these and many other difficulties. . . I shall most religiously believe that the finger of Providence is in it, to blind the eyes of our enemies; for surely if we get well through this month, it must be for want of their knowing[33] the disadvantages we labor under. (To Lieutenant Colonel Joseph Reed, 14 January 1776. *PGW*, Revolutionary War Series, vol. pp. 87–92.)

If my endeavors to avert the evil with which this country was threatened (by a deliberate plan of tyranny) should be crowned with the success that is wished, the praise is due to The Grand Architect of the universe who did not see fit to suffer His superstructures and justice to be subjected to the ambition of the princes of this world, or to the rod of oppression, in the hands of any power upon Earth. (To Elkanah Watson, August 10, 1782. *Founders Online*, National Archives.)

God's Ways Are Higher Than Ours. I look upon every dispensation of Providence as designed to answer some valuable purpose, and I hope I shall always possess a sufficient degree of fortitude to bare without murmuring any stroke which may happen either to my person or my estate from that quarter.

But I cannot with any degree of patience, behold the infamous practices of speculators, monopolizers, and all that ... are putting the rights and liberties of this country into the most eminent danger.

(To Lund Washington, May 29, 1779. *PGW*, Revolutionary War Series, vol. 20, pp. 688–690.)

Treason is Cowardice.   [Bring] those murderers of our cause—the monopolizers, forestallers and engrossers—to condign[34] punishment. It is much to be lamented that each State. . . has not hunted them down as the pests of society and the greatest enemies we have, to the happiness of America.

I would to God that one of the most atrocious in each state was hung in gibbets, up on a gallows five times as high as the one prepared by Haman. No punishment, in my opinion, is too great for the man who can build "his greatness upon his country's ruin." (To Joseph Reed, December 12, 1778. *PGW*, Revolutionary War Series, vol. 18, pp. 396–398.)

Faith Without Works Is Dead.   To trust altogether in the justice of our cause without our own utmost exertions, would be tempting Providence. (To Jonathan Trumbull, Sr., August 7, 1776. *PGW*, Revolutionary War Series, vol. 5, pp. 615–616.)

Internal Dissensions. I am under more apprehensions on account of our *own* dissensions than of the efforts of the enemy. (To Benedict Arnold, *The Writings of George Washington,* ed. Fitzpatrick 13:393.)

PERSONAL REFLECTIONS OF WAR

God's Hand During the American Revolution.
The Power and Goodness of the Almighty were strongly manifested in the events of our late glorious revolution, and His kind interposition in our behalf has been no less visible in the establishment of our present equal government.

In war, He directed the sword. And in peace, He has ruled in our councils. My agency in both has been guided by the best intentions, and a sense of the duty which I owe my Country. (To the Hebrew Congregations of the Eastern States, 13 December 1790. *PGW*, Presidential Series, vol. 7, pp. 61–64.)

When I contemplate the interposition[35] of Providence as it was visibly manifested in guiding us through the Revolution... I feel myself oppressed and almost overwhelmed with a sense of the divine munificence.[36] I feel that nothing is due to my personal agency in all these complicated and wonderful events, except what can simply be attributed to the exertions of an honest zeal for the good of my country. (To the Common Council of Philadelphia, 1789. *PGW*, Presidential Series, vol. 2, pp. 83-84)

With vows for the peace, the happiness, and prosperity of a country in whose service the prime of my life hath been spent, and with best wishes for the tranquility of all nations, and all men, the scene will close; grateful to that Providence which has directed my steps, and shielded me in the various changes and chances through which I have passed, from my youth to the present moment. (To William Gordon, 15 October 1797. *PGW*, Retirement Series, vol. 1, pp. 406–409.)

I am naturally led to reflect on the unlimited gratitude which we owe, as a nation, to the Supreme Arbiter[37] of human events for his interposition in our favor. (To the Georgia Legislature, 18 March 1790. *PGW*, Presidential Series, vol. 4, pp. 457–459.)

A contemplation of the complete attainment. . . of the object for which we contended (America), against so formidable a power, cannot but inspire us with astonishment and gratitude.

The disadvantageous circumstances on our part under which the war was undertaken can never be forgotten. The singular interpositions of Providence in our feeble condition were such as could scarcely escape the attention of the most unobserving, while the unparalleled perseverance of the armies of the United States, through almost every possible suffering and discouragement, for the space of eight long years, was little short of a standing miracle. (Farewell Address to the Army, 2 November 1783.)

I am sure there never was a people who had more reason to acknowledge a divine interposition in their affairs than those of the United States.

And I should be pained to believe that they have forgotten that Agency which was so often manifested during our Revolution, or that they failed to consider the omnipotence of that God who is alone able to protect them. (To John Armstrong, 11 March 1792. *PGW*, Presidential Series, vol. 10, pp. 85–87.)

The American Revolution *Designed* to Glorify God. We ought not to look back unless it is to derive useful lessons from past errors, and for the purpose of profiting. . . To [dwell upon] things that are past and irremediable[38] is unpleasing. But to steer clear of the shelves and rocks we have struck upon is the part of wisdom.

Our affairs are brought to an awful crisis *[so] that* the hand of Providence, I trust, may be more conspicuous in our deliverance.

The many remarkable interpositions of the divine. . . in the hours of our deepest distress and darkness have been too luminous to suffer me to doubt. (To John Armstrong, 26 March 1781. *Founders Online,* National Archives.)

Ours is a kind of struggle *designed*, I dare say, by Providence to try the patience, fortitude and virtue of Men. None, therefore, that are engaged in it will suffer themselves. . . to sink under difficulties or be discouraged by hardships. (To Andrew Lewis, 15 October 1778. *PGW*, Revolutionary War Series, 17:388–390.)

Principled Citizens Defend Liberty.   When everything sacred and dear to freemen is thus threatened, I could not, consistent with the principles which have actuated me through life, remain an idle spectator and refuse to obey the call of my country to lead its armies for defense and therefore have pledged myself to come forward whenever the exigency[39] shall require it. (To James Anderson, July 25, 1798. *PGW,* Retirement Series, vol. 2, pp. 452–454.)

Divinely Protected.   By the all-powerful dispensations[40] of Providence, I have been protected beyond all human probability or expectation. For I had 4 bullets through my coat, and 2 horses shot under me, yet escaped unhurt, although death was leveling my companions on every side of me. (To

John Augustine Washington, 1755. *PGW*, Colonial Series, vol. 1, p. 343.)

To say nothing of the invisible workings of Providence, which has conducted us through difficulties where no human foresight could point the way. . . It will appear evident to a close examiner, that there has been a concatenation[41] of causes to produce this event. Which, in all probability, at no time or under other circumstances, will combine again.

We deceive ourselves therefore by the mode of reasoning, and what would be much worse, we may bring ruin upon ourselves by attempting to carry it into practice. (To William Gordon, 8 July 1783. *Founders Online,* National Archives.)

Give Thanks and Glory to God. Glorious indeed has been our contest; glorious, if we consider the prize for which we have contended. But in the midst of our joys, I hope we shall not forget that to Divine Providence is to be ascribed the glory and the praise. (From George Washington to John

Rodgers, June 11, 1783.)

The success, which has hitherto attended our united efforts, we owe to the gracious interposition of Heaven, and to that interposition let us gratefully ascribe the praise of victory, and the blessings of peace. (To the Governor and Legislature of N.H, 3 November 1789. *PGW*, Presidential Series, vol. 4, pp. 277–278.)

On this happy occasion, suffer me. . . to join you in grateful adoration to that Divine Providence which hath rescued our country from the brink of destruction, [and] which hath crowned our exertions with the fairest fruits of success, and which now, instead of the anxiety and distress occasioned by perpetual[42] alarms, permits you to enjoy, without molestation, the sweets of peace and domestic happiness.

May a spirit of wisdom and rectitude[43] preside over all our councils and actions, and dispose us as a nation to avail ourselves of the blessings which are placed before us. Then shall we be happy indeed. (To Elias Dayton, 21 August 1783. *Founders Online,* National Archives.)

[I] acknowledge publicly our infinite obligations to the Supreme Ruler of the Universe for rescuing our Country from the brink of destruction.

I cannot fail at this time to ascribe all the honor of our late successes to the same glorious Being. And if my humble exertions have been made in any degree subservient[44] to the execution of the divine purposes, the contemplation[45] of the benediction of Heaven on our righteous Cause, the approbation of my virtuous Countrymen, and the testimony of my own conscience will be a sufficient reward. [This would] augment my felicity[46] beyond anything which the world can bestow. (To Johann Daniel Gros, 27 November 1783. *Founders Online,* National Archives.)

The Wicked Ignore God's Hand.   The man must be bad indeed, who can look up on the events of the American Revolution without feeling the warmest gratitude towards The Great Author of the universe, whose divine interposition was so frequently manifested in our behalf. (To Samuel Langdon, September 28, 1789. *PGW*, Presidential Series, vol. 4, p. 106.)

A Few Good Men. It is much easier at all times to prevent an evil than to rectify mistakes. It is infinitely better to have a few good men [in an army] than many indifferent ones. (To James McHenry, 10 August 1798. *PGW*, Retirement Series, vol. 2, pp. 508–511.)

THE CONSTITUTION

I now feel myself inexpressibly happy in a belief, that Heaven which has done so much for our infant Nation will not withdraw its Providential influence before our *political* felicity shall have been completed...

Thus supported by a firm trust in the great Arbiter of the Universe, aided by the collected wisdom of the union, and imploring the Divine benediction on our joint exertions in the service of our country, I readily engage with you in the arduous, but pleasing, task of attempting to make a nation happy. (To the Senate, [18 May] 1789. *The Papers of James Madison*, 12:166–167.)

Seek Direction From On High. The kind interposition of Providence which has been so often manifested in the affairs of this Country must naturally lead us to look up to that divine source for light and direction in this new and untried scene. (To William Heath, 9 May 1789. *PGW*, Presidential Series, vol. 2, p. 238.)

If, to please the people, we offer what we ourselves disapprove, how can we afterwards defend our work? Let us raise a standard to which the wise and the honest can repair. The event is in the hand of God. (To the delegates at the Constitutional Convention. *The Records of the Federal Convention of 1787*, Max Ferrand, ed.)

Miraculous Adoption of The Constitution. We have still good hopes of its adoption here... The plot thickens fast. A few short weeks will determine the political fate of America for the present generation, and probably produce no small influence on the happiness of society through a long succession of ages to come.

Should everything proceed with harmony and consent according to our actual wishes and expectations. it will be so much beyond anything we had a right to imagine or expect... It will demonstrate as visibly the finger of Providence as any possible event in the course of human affairs. (To Marquis de Lafayette, 28 May 1788. *PGW*, Confederation Series, vol. 6, pp. 297–299.)

It appears to me... little short of a miracle that the delegates from so many different states (which states, you know, are also different from each other in their manners, circumstances, and prejudices) should unite in forming a system of national government... (To Marquis de Lafayette, 7 February 1788. *PGW*, Confederation Series, vol. 6, pp. 95–98.)

Providence Preserved the Union. No one can rejoice more than I do at every step taken by the people of this great country to preserve the Union, establish good order and government, and to render the nation happy at home and respected abroad. No country upon Earth ever had it more in its power to attain these blessings than United America.

Wondrously strange then... would it be were we to neglect the means, and to stray from the road to which the finger of Providence has so manifestly pointed. I cannot believe it will ever come to pass!

The great Author of all good has not conducted us so far on the road to happiness and glory,
to withdraw from us in the hour of need...

By folly and misconduct... we may now and
then get bewildered, but I hope and trust that there
is good sense and virtue enough left [in the people]
to bring us back into the right way before we shall
be entirely lost. (To Benjamin Lincoln, 29 June
1788. *PGW*, Confederation Series, vol. 6, pp. 365–
366.)

**Internal Threats More Harmful Than Exter-
nal.** How unfortunate, and how much is it to be re-
gretted then, that whilst we are encompassed on all
sides with avowed enemies and insidious friends,
that *internal* dissentions should be harrowing and
tearing our vitals. The last, to me, is the most ser-
ious, the most alarming, and the most afflicting of
the two.

And without more charity for the opinions
and acts of one another in governmental matters...

I believe it will be difficult, if not impracticable, to manage the reins of government or to keep the parts of it together.

For if, instead of laying our shoulders to the machine after measures are decided on, one pulls this way and another that, before the utility of the thing is fairly tried, it must inevitably be torn asunder. And, in my opinion the fairest prospect of happiness and prosperity that ever was presented to man, will be lost, perhaps for ever! (To Thomas Jefferson, 23 August 1792. *The Papers of Thomas Jefferson*, vol. 24, pp. 315–319.)

Religious Freedom Forever Protected Under Constitution. If I could have entertained the slightest apprehension that the Constitution framed in the Convention, where I had the honor to preside, might possibly endanger the religious rights of any ecclesiastical Society, certainly I would never have placed my signature to it.

And if I could now conceive that the general government might ever be so administered as to render the liberty of conscience insecure, I beg you will be persuaded that *no one* would be more zealous than myself to establish effectual barriers against the horrors of *spiritual tyranny* and every species of religious persecution.

Remember that I have often expressed my sentiment, that every man, conducting himself as a good citizen, and being accountable to God alone for his religious opinions, ought to be protected in worshipping the Deity according to the dictates of his own conscience. (To the United Baptist Churches of Virginia, May 1789. *PGW,* Presidential Series, 2:423–425.)

DEFINITIONS

[1] **providential agency** – divine design

[2] **pious exaltation** – sacred joy or excitement

[3] **felicity** – happiness

[4] **gale** – storm or hurricane

[5] **turned my eye** – looked towards or trusted in

[6] **consummation** – completion or perfection

[7] **meliorating** – uplifting or edifying

[8] **have a disposition** – want or desire

[9] **wholesome** – morally correct or virtuous

[10] **meanderings** – unforeseen twists and turns

[11] **salutary**– valuable or beneficial

[12] **exult** - rejoice

[13] **profligate** – wicked; lost, broken, or ruined in regards to morality

[14] **favor** – kindness or support

[15] **vindicating** – defending or supporting

[16] **province** – state

[17] **contracted** – formed

[18] **indelible** – deeply rooted or hard to break

[19] **factious** – contention and separation

[20] **indigent** – needy

[21] **give every furtherance** – completely support

[22] **faction** – cliques or party politics

[23] **want** – lack

[24] **gaming** – games of chance involving money; gambling.

[25] **vice and dissipation** – wickedness

[26] **impiety and folly** – immorality, lightmindedness and stupidity

[27] **despairing** – weary or hopeless

[28] **base art** – shameful or wicked practice; temptation

[29] **garrison** – body of troops

[30] **perfidy** – treachery or disloyalty

[31] **it behooves us to supplicate** – we should earnestly seek or desire

[32] **rise superior to** – overcome

[33] **for want of their knowing** – because they don't know

[34] **condign** – appropriate or well deserved

[35] **interposition** – involvement or guidance

[36] **munificence** – generosity or kindness

[37] **arbiter** – judge or mediator

[38] **irremediable** – permanent or irreversible

[39] **exigency** – situation

[40] **dispensations** – decree or design

[41] **concatenation** – sequence or chain; unlikely series

[42] **perpetual** – continuous

[43] **rectitude** – righteousness

[44] **subservient** – useful

[45] **contemplation** –recognition or remembrance

[46] **augment my felicity** – bring me joy

ABOUT THE AUTHOR

Ezra Vaoifi

Ezra grew up in Independ-
ence, MO. After returning
home from a 2 year mis-
sion trip for The Church
of Jesus Christ of Latter-
Day Saints, Ezra met his
wife Sabrina and they
were married in 2018.

Ezra is an entrepreneur
and a lover of American History. He attends Brig-
ham Young University with his wife in Provo, Utah.
His religious roots and fascination with the American Revolution were the origin of this book.

Contact him anytime at ezravaoifi2@gmail.com.

Made in the USA
Columbia, SC
06 July 2023

20111018R00055